CRISIS

INTERVENTION

STRATEGIES FOR CHEMICAL ABUSERS AND OFFENDERS

Gregory L. Little, ED.D., LPC

Kenneth D. Robinson, ED.D., CPC

Katherine D. Burnette, M.S., LAODAC

EAGLE WING BOOKS, INC.
Memphis, Tennessee

CRISIS INTERVENTION
STRATEGIES FOR CHEMICAL ABUSERS AND OFFENDERS

Printed in the United States of America.

Published by
Eagle Wing Books, Inc.
P.O. Box 9972
Memphis, TN 38190

ISBN: 0-940829-20-7

Retail price: $10.00

DEDICATION

To

William H. Welch

Professor, teacher, colleague, friend.
Gone, but never forgotten, as your influence
continues in countless others.

TABLE OF CONTENTS

History 1

Important Crisis Factors 4

Modern Views Of Crisis Theory 6
    Equilibrium Model 6
    Cognitive Model 6
    Psychosocial Transition Model 7
    Eclectic Crisis Intervention 7

Crisis Intervention Defined 7
    Crisis Intervention For Chemical Abusers 8
    Crisis Intervention For Offenders 8

What Is A Crisis? 9

Factors Underlying Crises 10

Crisis Terms & Conditions 10
    Hazardous Event/Situation 10
    Precipitating Event 11
    Vulnerability 11
    The Final Straw 11
    Active Crisis 12

Crisis Stages 12
    Stage 1 12
    Stage 2 13
    Stage 3 13
    Stage 4 13

Life Stressors 14

Offender Stressors 16

Outside Events That Can Cause Stress 18
Inside Events That Can Cause Stress 19

Crisis Intervention Counseling 20
Stage 1 — Crisis Recognition 20
Stage 2 — Define The Problem 21
Stage 3 — Assist In The Setting of a Limited Goal ... 23
Stage 4 — Beginning Problem Solving Efforts 27
Stage 5 — Focused Problem Solving 30

Specific Crisis Issues Frequently Encountered 32
Medical Emergencies (Overdose) 32
Violent Clients 32
Predictors of Violence 33
Depression/Suicidal Clients 34
Relapse 35
Job Loss - Financial Problems 36
Death of a Loved One - Serious Illness 37
Loss of an Important Relationship 38

Offender Crises 39
Adjustment to Incarceration 39
Fear/Threats 39
Problems With Staff 40
Parole/Probation Loss 42

References 43

Appendix A — Crisis Intervention Guide Forms 45

Appendix B — Anxiety & Depression Scales 53
Anxiety Status Inventory 54
Depression Status Inventory 56

Index 58

About The Authors 61

HISTORY

The history of crisis intervention is long and detailed and a thorough examination would require a text in itself. Thus, only a cursory review of crisis intervention's history is presented here.

The acknowledged origin of crisis intervention comes from Erich Lindemann's (1944) study of grief reactions of 101 persons who were coping with the recent death of a relative. Many of Lindemann's subjects were relatives of the famous 1942 Coconut Grove nightclub fire in Boston that killed nearly 500 people. Lindemann found that grief responses were predictable and progressed through a distinct series of stages and that they were "normal reactions." In general, such reactions had a distinct onset (the death of a loved one), showed acute symptoms, and lasted for relatively brief periods. While a minority of people experiencing grief developed serious psychopathology, most people went through transitory struggles in an attempt to adjust to the new situation. Lindemann surmised that by intervening with specific counseling techniques, individuals experiencing the grief could make the necessary adjustments more readily and resist the development of more serious problems. Lindemann suggested that attempting to help clients understand what was happening to them, identify the tasks they were facing, and then master these tasks would facilitate the healing process and prevent more serious pathology from developing. Thus, Lindemann called his approach *preventive intervention.*

In 1948 Lindemann created the Wellesley Human Relations Service in Massachusetts, a forerunner of modern mental health centers, to test his theories. One of the many colleagues Lindemann had at Wellesley was Gerald Caplan. Caplan revised Lindemann's early ideas about crises and incorporated Erik Erikson's idea of developmental crises into the emerging theoretical framework. Caplan (1960; 1964) devised a crisis theory based on *homeostasis*, the idea that situations and events can upset the delicate balance of an individual's emotional and mental functioning. The essence of Caplan's approach is still used in crisis intervention today.

Caplan theorized that as a person's homeostasis became unbalanced by upsetting events or threats, the individual employed their typical problem solving strategies. Although there is tension and anxiety during the crisis, once the person mastered the problem, the tension dissipated. Caplan observed that most crises were short in duration (one to five weeks), but if the person found that their typical problem solving methods didn't work, a true crisis emerged increasing the tension.

Caplan viewed crises as the individual's emotional re-action rather than the event or situation precipitating the problem. Caplan further divided crises into two types — **developmental** and **accidental**. A key to understanding crisis, in this view, was the person's *interpretation* of the situation as significant or of critical importance and how well prepared the person was to handle the situation. In short, some people are better able to resolve crises satisfactorily because of their prior experience and certain personality factors.

Caplan found **four** distinct stages of crises. The *first stage* occurs when a person finds that important needs are threatened resulting in the person trying to solve the problem with their usual methods. If the person is unable to cope utilizing their usual methods, the *second stage* of crisis develops. In this stage,

---

Caplan viewed crises as the individual's emotional reaction rather than the event or situation precipitating the problem.

increased tension and anxiety occur followed by a gradual deterioration of the individual and frantic "trial and error" efforts at solving the problem. During this stage and lasting throughout the remainder of the crisis, the person tends to seek out help and shows a willingness to accept assistance from others. The *third stage* follows failure of the trial and error methods with a further increase in tension resulting in a state of emotional emergency. Some people are able to solve the problem using novel methods or through assistance while others simply accept the problem ending the crisis. However, for those who don't solve or accept the crisis, they move into the *fourth stage* which Caplan called the "breaking point." The fourth stage is marked by a deterioration of personality.

Caplan observed that some persons were particularly prone to personality deterioration, especially those who had ongoing mental disorders and others who had previously deteriorated during crises. Caplan viewed crisis as a "struggle to adapt" and people emerged from crises either more or less mentally able to handle future crises.

Caplan observed that some persons were particularly prone to personality deterioration, especially those who had ongoing mental disorders and others who had previously deteriorated during crises.

Important Crisis Factors

Various factors have been found to be important and significant in crises. Some crises occur in the context of a person's **social group**, for example, the individual's **family**. It is frequently observed that families undergoing a crisis created by a loss **willingly accept outside help more so than at other times** (Parad & Caplan, 1960; Rapoport, 1962; Waldfogel & Gardner, 1961). Rapoport (1962) found that **many crises directly related to an individual's past experience with threats and could stimulate ongoing unresolved conflicts.** Thus, counselors treating clients during crises may find clients relating their present crisis to past events.

Since the development of crisis theory in the 1950s and 1960s, many clinicians have researched and verified most of the earlier findings and refined techniques. Only a brief review of these findings is presented here.

Some clinicians view crisis intervention as a **brief psychotherapy** (Butcher & Maudal, 1976; Patterson & O'Sullivan, 1974) where *every session should be approached as if it may be the last session.* In addition, it is generally agreed that crisis

---

Some clinicians view crisis intervention as a brief psychotherapy ...where every session should be approached as if it may be the last session. In addition, it is generally agreed that crisis intervention treatments should be initiated quickly...

---

intervention treatments should be initiated quickly (Waldfogel & Gardner, 1961; Shaw, Blumenfeld, & Senf, 1968). Early research also showed that effective crisis intervention could be conducted in 3 - 12 sessions (Patterson & O'Sullivan, 1974) and that *involvement of family and significant others could increase effectiveness* (Ewalt, 1973; Butcher & Maudal, 1976). In addition, the conditions creating crisis have been found to be a wide-ranging possible set of circumstances (Lang, 1974; Wolkon, 1972) but that *the focus of the crisis intervention itself should be on the presenting problem* — especially the precipitating event (Hoffman & Remmel, 1975). Asking the question, "Why now?" is important in crisis intervention strategies.

Another underlying theme uncovered by the earlier crisis intervention research was that crisis intervention should have *strengthening the client's ability to deal with future crises* as a major goal (Kaffman, 1963; Berlin, 1970). Furthermore, crisis intervention should not give the client a sense of "false hopes" but rather a **realistic** picture of the situation and its consequences (Butcher & Maudal, 1976; Schwartz, 1971). Thus, it has been argued that *crisis intervention is an active, directive, and pragmatic approach to problem-solving* (Patterson & O'Sullivan, 1974; Kaffman, 1963). Finally, many researchers have found that *clients who achieve positive results from crisis intervention treatment have a tendency to be more amenable to longer-term therapeutic efforts* (Hoffman & Remmel, 1975; Kardener, 1975).

...crisis intervention should have strengthening the client's ability to deal with future crises as a major goal... Furthermore, crisis intervention should not give the client a sense of "false hopes" but rather a realistic picture of the situation and its consequences...

More Modern Views of Crisis Theory

Modern texts describe four basic models of crisis intervention theory (Gilliland, & James, 1988) with their frameworks derived from earlier research.

Equilibrium Model

As outlined by Caplan (1960; 1964), the equilibrium model asserts that patients enter crises when their equilibrium becomes unbalanced by internal or external events. Their typical responses to situations seem to be ineffective leading to increased tension and anxiety which, in turn, creates greater loss of equilibrium. The primary goal of this model is to reestablish balance and equilibrium by focusing on the precipitating factors of the crisis. Almost all crisis intervention techniques begin by first attempting to uncover precipitating factors and assist clients in finding effective coping strategies. The precipitating factor is sometimes viewed as "the straw that broke the camel's back" (Hoffman & Remmel 1975).

Cognitive Model

One of the earliest critics of the equilibrium crisis model was Taplin (1971). Taplin argued that rather than simply being a reactor to outside events, people *perceived* and *evaluated* potentially disruptive situations on a "cognitive" level that interrupted their normal thinking ability. Bartolucci and Drayer (1973) also made the same observations and stated that the manner in which an individual views events was a key. The cognitive model seeks to change a client's irrational beliefs and faulty thinking about the situation.

Psychosocial Transition Model

The psychosocial transition model draws from Erik Erikson's theories of developmental life stages and transitions. As related earlier, Caplan found that two types of crises tended to present themselves. These were **accidental** (brought on by precipitating outside events) and **developmental**. The developmental model recognizes that humans are constantly developing and evolving as they move from one life stage to another, and that the interaction between external and internal changes can lead to crises. The goal of developmental crises intervention models is to assist the person to make appropriate adaptations to developmental changes.

Eclectic Crisis Intervention

The eclectic crisis intervention approach is a "hybrid" derived from elements of other models (Gilliland & James, 1988). Substance abuse counselor guidelines tend to primarily utilize the eclectic model rather than focusing on only one of the theoretical frameworks. The eclectic model recognizes all three of the other approaches as relevant and useful and employs methods from all of them as appropriate. An eclectic approach is presented in this text.

Crisis Intervention Defined

Crisis intervention is an active, directive, and pragmatic approach to problem-solving that is quickly and therapeutically utilized when a client experiences acute emotional or physical distress due to a crisis.

Crisis Intervention for Chemical Abusers

When chemical abusers in treatment experience crises, all of the gains realized from treatment and rehabilitative efforts are at risk. The risk of relapse, overdose, suicide, acting out and other destructive behavior, and withdrawal from treatment all escalate. *The primary goal of crisis intervention for chemical abusers in treatment is to protect and enhance the overall rehabilitation gains.* Thus, identification of the important precipitating problems or difficulties causing the crisis is the first step. Reduction or elimination of the precipitating problem is the second step of crisis intervention combined with efforts to alleviate the anxiety and tension in the client. Finally, attempts should be made to use the crisis resolution to strengthen the client's chemical abuse treatment gains and provide resilience in future crises.

Crisis Intervention for Offenders

Offenders in crises tend to become emotionally and behaviorally unstable leading to possible destructive behavior to self and others. The risk of violence or avoidance behavior is increased. For example, offenders on work release have absconded at times when they discovered that their "significant other" was dating someone else. Offenders on probation have been known to perform numerous crimes after being arrested (and subsequently released on bail) for petty crimes. DWI arrestees are at a high risk for suicidal behavior and gestures (and for more DWIs) in the immediate time period after arrest and/or release.

The primary goal of crisis intervention for chemical abusers in treatment is to protect and enhance the overall rehabilitation gains.

What Is A Crisis?

With chemical abusers in treatment, *a crisis is an important, critical occurrence that presents a hazard to the overall stability and sobriety of the client.* Typically, a client experiences overwhelming emotional pressure and stress during a crisis that impairs their ability to employ appropriate problem-solving. Counselors should understand that during crises, people tend to "fall back on" their usual coping methods. For alcoholics, this can mean the use of alcohol. For drug abusers, the use of drugs is a risk. *Relapse is a major risk during a crisis.* It is also important to recognize that relapse itself can precipitate a crisis in substance abuse clients.

Offenders experience crises from numerous factors and events. Incarcerated offenders often see outside events as out of their control and will sometimes take desperate measures to exert whatever control they believe they can. Parole and probation hearings, program and housing assignment changes, health conditions, and numerous internal and external forces can precipitate crises. Changes in the health and physical conditions of significant others "on the outside" (free world) cause emotional reactions in the incarcerated and many offenders experience significant guilt reactions that can lead to desperate behavior. A goal of crisis intervention with offenders is to maintain the health, safety, and well-being of the individual and others.

...a crisis is an important, critical occurrence that presents a hazard to the overall stability and sobriety of the client.

Factors Underlying Crises

Crises are characterized by a number of important markers. These markers are factors underlying how the person perceives the situation and include:

- **Viewing the problem as overwhelming**

- **Seeing the problem as extremely important**

- **Feeling vulnerable or weak at the time of the crisis**

- **Feeling unprepared**

- **Typical coping strategies don't work**

- **Support systems don't help or aren't available**

Crisis Terms & Conditions

Several terms are useful in analyzing crises. These terms have long been employed to understand and cope with crises and counselors should be familiar with each.

Hazardous Event/Situation.

This can be a sequence of events that makes the individual vulnerable to crisis. Thus, a serious situation or occurrence can seem unbearable to a person coping with a hazardous chain of events. A substance abuser in treatment may have been struggling to hold all areas of his life together for some time. This can be seen as a hazardous event — a chain of events tied together — that presents a hazard or leads to vulnerability.

Precipitating Event.

The precipitating event is sometimes seen as the first or final occurrence "causing" or stimulating the crisis. It typically occurs at the end of the chain of events called the hazardous event and is experienced as the "final straw." It is seen as a serious *hazard* to the social/emotional/physical health of the person and is also viewed as very important. It is often acute, sudden, and unforeseen and is seen as unbearable or intolerable. For example, the death of a loved one, loss of job, or loss of freedom can all be precipitating events. A later section addresses hazards and life stressors.

Vulnerability.

At the time of the precipitating event, *the individual feels unable to deal with the precipitating event* and is therefore vulnerable. They may feel emotionally and physically weak or have other vulnerabilities. For example, having no money or insurance after being told that one has a serious disease can be seen as being vulnerable. Clients entering drug treatment often feel vulnerable for various reasons including having others discover the depth of their problem, loss of job or status, and even from the possibility of having drug urine screens taken.

The Final Straw.

Sometimes the precipitating event itself can be viewed as the final straw but, often after problem-solving efforts fail to resolve the problem, another event (even small events) can occur that makes the person feel totally *helpless*.

Active Crisis.

When the client is in the crisis itself it is said to be active. During this time, the individual is most amenable to outside assistance and intervention. The individual is typically anxious and tense, indecisive, and desperate. They may feel a sense of doom and hopelessness.

Crisis Stages

Crises progress through predictable stages that have been delineated by research. Crises typically are short in duration lasting from a few hours to perhaps six weeks. In addition, during crises, individuals tend to be more amenable to outside help and sometimes willingly and actively seek outside help. Although there are several theoretical models of the stages of crisis, most recognize four distinct stages each with hazards and risks.

Stage 1 — A precipitating event (final straw) occurs causing distress that leads to the individual employing their usual problem-solving methods. This occurs at a time of vulnerability after a chain of hazardous events. Note that some chemical abusers can relapse almost immediately here, especially those in the very beginning of treatment. Offenders

Crises progress through predictable stages that have been delineated by research. Crises typically are short in duration lasting from a few hours to perhaps six weeks.

prone to violence may resort to violent means to resolve the problem. In cases of immediate relapse or violence, the immediate crisis may dissipate, but, of course, a new set of conditions presents itself possibly leading to another crisis.

Stage 2 — If the usual problem-solving strategy fails to resolve the crisis, anxiety and tension immediately increase thereby increasing the intensity of the crisis.

Stage 3 — In response to the increasing tension from failed efforts to solve the problem, the individual can turn to trial and error attempts to solve the problem. Acts of desperation, irrational behavior, and occasionally effective problem-solving occur in this stage. However, when efforts fail, the person progresses to the final stage.

Stage 4 — In the final stage of crises, the person essentially gives up. In situations where the individual truly has no control, the adage "let go and let God" may be appropriate and the serenity prayer can be comforting. However, the person may not have attempted appropriate problem-solving behaviors and is probably not aware of all of the possibilities and opportunities. For many substance abusers, "giving up" may mean return to use. "What is the use of trying to change," many will say to themselves as they relapse.

In the final stage of crises, the person essentially gives up. In situations where the individual truly has no control, the adage "let go and let God" may be appropriate

Life Stressors

In 1963, Dr. Richard Rahe developed a scale assessing events in life that caused stress for "normal" persons. In 1978, Dr. Rahe revised the scale and assigned points for various life events. A modified version of Rahe's scale is listed below (adapted from *Recovery Times* article, June 1991). Points are assigned based on the event happening within the past 12 months and added. For example, an offender who is incarcerated (57 points), lost his job (64 points), has a pregnant wife (60 points), has experienced financial ruin (30 points), and is having trouble adjusting to the jail routine (30 points) has a total of 241 points. This indicates a moderate life crisis based on Rahe's scale.

A substance abuser in treatment may be experiencing a divorce or separation (62 points) from a pregnant "wife" (60 points), arguments with a significant other (30 points), illness or weakness from substance abuse (30 points), changes in finances (30 points), have recently taken out a large car loan (30 points), experiencing problems with in-laws (30 points), having problems in sleep and changing drug usage habits (30 points), a sick father (52 points), and problems with his boss (30 points) totalling 384 points. This indicates a relatively high degree of stress. If his mother died (adding 65 points), the total would escalate to 449. The client, already experiencing high stress, could view the mother's death as a "final straw" precipitating a major life crisis.

The Life Stress Scale asserts that a total of 200 - 400 points indicates minor to moderate life crises. Totals over 400 points indicate major life crises. While the scale provides counselors with a way of assessing the relative weight of possible life stressors, it is important to understand that it may not be a valid or accurate assessment tool. Its greatest use may be in seeing how various events can accumulate in a person's life precipitating crises. Just being in treatment represents a change for clients thereby increasing stress. Many of the life stressors (with assigned points) are listed below. (Points are assigned if the condition is currently present or has been present within the last year.)

- Death of spouse or significant other — 105
- Death of close family member — 65
- Fired from job — 64
- Divorce — 62
- Pregnancy — 60
- Incarceration — 57
- Foreclosure, loss of home — 57
- Separation in Marriage/Relationship — 56
- Health change in family member — 52
- Getting married — 50
- New family member — 50
- Sex problems — 49
- Retiring from work — 49
- A close friend's death — 46
- Illness/injury — 30
- Financial change — 30
- Career change — 30
- New loan — 30
- More/less arguments with significant other — 30
- Child leaves home — 30
- Problems with in-laws — 30
- Change in significant other's work — 30
- In or out of school — 30
- Problems with boss/supervisor — 30
- Change in work hours — 30
- Changing residence — 30
- Changing schools — 30
- Change in sleep habits — 30
- Change in personal habits — 30

Offender Stressors

Offenders face numerous, ongoing stressors. One of the most valid and frequent observations with those incarcerated is that immediately after incarceration a *usually* temporary depression ensues. Stress and anxiety increase due to major life changes in virtually all life areas. Housing conditions immediately change. Sharing sleeping and living space with others —

One of the most valid and frequent observations with those incarcerated is that immediately after incarceration a usually temporary depression ensues. Stress and anxiety increase ... Housing conditions immediately change. Sharing sleeping and living space with others — usually totally outside of the offender's control — occurs. Eating habits, sleeping schedules and conditions, all daily routines, clothing, hygiene, and personal time habits all are subject to uncontrollable changes. A sense of loss of personal control is often experienced ... Depression, anxiety disorders, and suicidal behaviors are risks with many offenders in the beginning of incarceration

usually totally outside of the offender's control — occurs. Eating habits, sleeping schedules and conditions, all daily routines, clothing, hygiene, and personal time habits all are subject to uncontrollable changes. A sense of loss of personal control is often experienced — especially at the beginning of incarceration. Depression, anxiety disorders, and suicidal behaviors are risks with many offenders in the beginning of incarceration. Jails that house DWI arrestees immediately after their arrest must be sensitive to the fact that suicide attempts are a very real possibility with such offenders.

Many institutions attempt to orient and stabilize the stresses on the newly incarcerated through systematic counseling contacts variously called "orientation" or "needs assessments" routinely performed as part of the intake process. Many institutions will assign those with the greatest risk as well as those showing significant and obvious impairments to special needs units. The maintenance of a "mental health unit" has been found helpful to stabilize those who are seriously depressed as well as those in need of ongoing mental health care (medications/support). Protective custody, suicide watch cells, and special housing units are often maintained for such clients.

Other situations frequently arise that cause stress in offenders and counselors should be aware of their occurrence and significance. For example, the authors know of inmates

The maintenance of a "mental health unit" has been found helpful to stabilize those who are seriously depressed as well as those in need of ongoing mental health care (medications/support).

who escaped from minimum security status to "talk to their girlfriend" to make sure she would "wait for their release." Of course, the escape itself led to increased stress due to a new sentence. In regards to assessing risks with offenders, it is important to keep in mind that the offender's *perception* of potential problems itself can lead to stress and the precipitation of crises. With offenders, a lot of crisis counseling consists of "what if" discussions. For example, "what if I don't get parole?" Offenders spend a great deal of time engaging in "what if" thinking, in part, due to their perceived lack of control over their situation. *Acceptance and adaptation to the incarceration is a major goal of crisis counseling with the incarcerated. Thus, crisis counseling often focuses on assisting the offender to successfully complete their incarceration with minimal problems and hopefully gain something beneficial from the experience.* Events both inside and outside the institution can contribute to the stress and subsequent crises of the incarcerated:

Outside Events That Can Cause Stress

- **Death of family member**
- **Death of friend**
- **Family problems from client's incarceration**
- **Family health problems**
- **Family financial problems**
- **Family living conditions threatened or changed**
- **Possible loss of loved one (fear of abandonment)**
- **Possible permanent job/career loss**
- **Fear of loss of outside support**
- **Pressure from outside acquaintances/cohorts**

Inside Events That Can Cause Stress

- Possibility of additional charges/sentence
- Loss of institutional privileges
- Threats from others — fear
- Fear of parole/probation denial
- Actual denial of parole/probation release
- Problems with particular staff members
- Illness/sickness
- Disciplinary infractions
- Changes in housing/living assignments
- Events that cause a loss of status/prestige
- Dismissal from important programming
- Change in counselor
- Difficulty adapting to institutional routines

...crisis counseling often focuses on assisting the offender to successfully complete their incarceration with minimal problems and hopefully gain something beneficial from the experience.

Crisis Intervention Counseling

Although there are many different styles and descriptions of crisis intervention stages, a "**generic**," basic series of five stages are described here. This is an eclectic model derived from equilibrium concepts and other models. There is some overlap to the stages and counselors may well combine some of the elements from each into various sessions. The number of sessions may vary depending upon the nature of the crisis as well as the client's personal characteristics, but the early sessions may last for an extended time. In general, the initial counseling sessions will occur with only a short period of time intervening (a few hours to a day or so). Since crises tend to be acute, it is important to recognize when clients are in them and to act quickly. Crisis intervention requires a rapid response. Thus, recognition of the client in crisis is the first stage in crisis intervention counseling.

Stage 1 — Crisis Recognition
Perhaps the majority of clients in crisis will make it known to counselors and other staff on their own. As stated repeatedly, people in crisis tend to be more amenable to help and will often seek out outside help in coping with their crisis. At other times, counselors may suspect a crisis based on client observations, program events, or through other clients. *Some signs of client crisis are emotional and behavioral reactions*

Since crises tend to be acute, it is important to recognize when clients are in them and to act quickly. Crisis intervention requires a rapid response.

---

that seem out of place or are problematic in and of themselves. For example, suicidal talk and gestures, violence, irrational or sudden mood swings, relapse, crying, or withdrawal all are common signs of crisis. Simply asking, *"what is going on?," "is there something I can do?,"* or *"would you like to talk about this?"* are all appropriate questions that can lead the client to share the problem.

In general, when clients experience crises, *it is best to talk to them in a one-on-one session* to facilitate safety and alleviate anxiety. If the client is around others and experiencing a crisis, moving them to a private area or office is appropriate. The goal of this intervention is to assist the client to take positive behavioral actions to resolve the crisis and *prevent relapse, injury, or further harm.* Simply engaging the client in a discussion and attending to their problem can provide some immediate relief. In addition, talking to the counselor about the problem represents a positive behavioral action by the client.

Stage 2 — Define The Problem

After the crisis is recognized and the client shows willingness to share the problem, the counselor seeks to define the problem (note that stages 1, 2, and 3 often occur in the same initial session). This means *listening* to the client's story, truly *understanding* what they say both *verbally* and through *nonverbal* behavior, and to let the client know that the counselor hears and understands. This may take some time and requires giving the client *feedback,* occasionally seeking *clarification,* and *restating* what the client says to validate that the counselor hears

---

understand what has caused the crisis, why the client feels vulnerable and unable to cope with it, and possible ramifications of the crisis

---

One major goal of this stage of crisis intervention is to identify the precipitating event so that both the client and counselor can clearly understand and see how the crisis was initiated.

and understands what is being said. The goal here is to understand *what has caused the crisis, why the client feels vulnerable and unable to cope with it, and possible ramifications of the crisis.* Counselors facilitate this by *asking simple, direct questions.*

One major goal of this stage of crisis intervention is to *identify the precipitating event* so that both the client and counselor can clearly understand and see how the crisis was initiated. Questions like, *"what brought on this crisis?," "how and when did this event occur?,"* and *"who else is involved?"* are all questions that should be asked. As the client responds to the questions, both verbal and nonverbal responses should be observed and assessed. With substance abusers, the possibility of client relapse is always an issue and it should be noted whether the client appears to be under the influence.

With potentially suicidal clients, once the counselor understands the problem and precipitating event, asking them three questions (or other versions of them) assesses suicide risk. These three questions are: *"How depressed are you?"* If the client states that they are depressed, ask, *"do you have a plan?"* Note that suicidal patients will almost always immediately recognize the question's intent (it means "do you know how you would kill yourself if you did it?"). Clients who have a plan present a greater risk than those who don't. The third question relates to the client's answer to the previous question. For example, if a client replies, "I would shoot myself," ask, *"do you have access to a gun"* or *"what gun would you use?"* Finding out if the elements of a potential suicide plan are available to the client (e.g., guns, pills for overdose, a car) are important and may require preventative actions on the part of the counselor.

Stage 3 — Assist In The Setting of a Limited Goal

After the client's precipitating event is understood and the counselor knows how this has affected the client, *a limited goal that is related to the problem and is easily attainable should be mutually set.* This allows the client to know that the counselor is helping him or her and also that the client can act to alleviate the crisis. The setting of a limited goal is accomplished for several other purposes. These include *averting a deeper crisis* (or averting a catastrophe) and bringing a sense of *balance* back into the client's life. In addition, the client will have a sense of *hope* and an *expectation* that they will emerge from the crisis.

In many cases, clients in crisis will feel guilt and feel responsible for what has occurred. At the same time, they may feel inadequate and hopeless. In such cases, clients need *respect*

With potentially suicidal clients, ... asking them three questions... assesses suicide risk. ...: "How depressed are you?" ... "do you have a plan?" ...Clients who have a plan present a greater risk than those who don't. The third question relates to the client's answer ... For example, if a client replies, "I would shoot myself," ask, "do you have access to a gun" or "what gun would you use?"

---

and *concern* rather than blame or guilt.

Examples of appropriate limited goals depend upon the client's specific problem. If a substance abuser in treatment has just found out that he lost his job, it might be suggested that he *make a list of his qualifications, job experiences, and educational background* before the next session. (Note that the next session should be as soon as possible — perhaps the next day in outpatient settings or later that day in an inpatient setting.) Others in treatment may agree to *attend a support group meeting* as their goal. *Writing a letter, making a call, making a list, or just agreeing to come back after lunch* (without relapsing) could all be appropriate as might *relaxation exercises* or other stress-reducing activities.

Counselors should understand that, while the goal formed in the session is mutually agreed, the counselor will probably have to suggest it and be fairly *directive*. Choose a goal that is reasonable, attainable, and related to the problem so that the client can feel like he or she is working toward a solution. With substance abusers and alcoholics, making it "one day at a time" should be kept in mind. Clients in crisis can exist day to day, hour to hour, minute to minute. Thus, *having a firm un-*

Counselors should understand that, while the goal formed in the session is mutually agreed, the counselor will probably have to suggest it and be fairly directive. Choose a goal that is reasonable, attainable, and related to the problem so that the client can feel like he or she is working toward a solution.

Remember that an overriding goal of the initial session is to protect the client, protect others, prevent relapse, and alleviate unbearable pressures.

derstanding of the goal, how and when it is to be accomplished, and when you will meet with them again should be pinned down.

Pinning down the accomplishment of the goal means that all of the details have been covered. How, where, what, and when are all specified. The counselor should ask specific sequential questions. For example, "what is the first thing you will do when you leave here?" "What time are you going to go to the bus stop to come back?" "When are you going to start working on this list?" "What time are you calling me?" "Where will you call me from?" "How will you get to your meeting tonight?"

If moving the client through the first three stages of crisis intervention sufficiently brings relief to the client, you can prepare the client for their next session. *Remember that an overriding goal of the initial session is to protect the client, protect others, prevent relapse, and alleviate unbearable pressures.* If this goal has been achieved, set another appointment time immediately after the goal is scheduled to be accomplished. While there is some flexibility with the next meeting, it should be *as soon as is possible* keeping in mind that some crises can be life-threatening and/or relapse producing. Counselors who are skilled in relaxation exercises and anxiety reducing methods may find these useful to employ at this time.

A goal for some suicidal clients can be a *suicide agree-*

ment with the counselor. This agreement confirms that the client will do nothing to harm themselves before meeting with the counselor again as well as agreeing to notify the counselor or other staff if their depression worsens. *Some understanding of the extent of a client's outside support is important here.* Clients who have much outside support should be encouraged to use it. At the same time, clients who have little or no outside support systems may present greater risks.

Clients with a poor support system need to know that they have ongoing support. That support may consist of solely you — their counselor. Provide the client with a means of contacting you in an emergency and provide them with specific written information regarding local agencies or other services that are appropriate for their problem. For suicidal patients, schedule phone appointments. Set limits on the time that you will allow for phone time. Tell them to call you when they get home or at a specific time. ("Call me at 7:00 tonight at this number.") Suicidal patients without outside support need

---

Some understanding of the extent of a client's outside support is important here. Clients who have much outside support should be encouraged to use it. At the same time, clients who have little or no outside support systems may present greater risks. Clients with a poor support system need to know that they have ongoing support. That support may consist of solely you — their counselor.

---

contact, thus, it is critical to return their calls immediately and follow through with agreements. As the crisis subsides, wait a small period of time (30 minutes or so) prior to returning their calls. This is a means of reducing dependency on you and gives the client time to process the problem. When it is appropriate, you should tell the client that they have the means to cope with their problem.

Stage 4 — Beginning Problem Solving Efforts & Support

With completion of the limited goal from the prior stage, many clients will experience a lessening of anxiety and tension. At the same time, *clients need ongoing encouragement and need to see that they have the ability to resolve and make it through the crisis.* At this time they may be better able to objectively view the crisis and provide more information. *How the crisis involves other people, how much it impacts the client's significant others, and the effects of the crisis on the client can be explored.* Once again, it is important to maintain the basic counseling approach of *listening and attending, restating and paraphrasing to validate the counselor's understanding of the problem, and allowing the client to express emotions and*

With completion of the limited goal from the prior stage, many clients will experience a lessening of anxiety and tension. At the same time, clients need ongoing encouragement and need to see that they have the ability to resolve and make it through the crisis.

---

feelings — these are critical elements in this counseling approach. *Helping the client to see the complete, nondistorted reality of the crisis is important.* In addition, it is important that the client understand that some feelings, emotional responses, and behaviors are *normal* during some crises. For example, it is normal for an offender to experience grief when a parent dies and perhaps to feel guilt. They may have a sense of desperation about not being able to attend the funeral or see other family members. That is normal. Some institutions can and do make provisions for offenders to attend a funeral while many others do not. If it is possible, the counselor should make appropriate efforts on the client's behalf.

One of the major goals of stage 4 is to bring a sense of balance or equilibrium back to the client. Just getting the client to objectively understand the entire problem can assist with this. If a client understands how he or she has responded to the

---

One of the major goals of stage 4 is to bring a sense of balance or equilibrium back to the client. Just getting the client to objectively understand the entire problem can assist with this. If a client understands how he or she has responded to the crisis, interacting with others involved, certain choices and options may become apparent. Exploring options and choices can be accomplished once clients have become less tense and anxious.

---

crisis, interacting with others involved, certain choices and options may become apparent. *Exploring options and choices can be accomplished once clients have become less tense and anxious.* At the same time, the client may begin to see how they have failed to utilize the social supports that they actually have. For example, many alcoholics may find that their crises tend to occur when they have reduced their attendance at support meetings and have little contact with their sponsor.

Stage 4 may occur over several sessions with exploration of the precipitating event, the series of "hazardous" events that led to the client's vulnerability, and the client's response. While crisis counseling needs to be controlled by the counselor, at this time it should be stressed to the client that it is a joint effort: "Let's see what we can do about this problem."

In this stage of counseling, the major focus of sessions will be on exploration of the current crisis, current support systems, client beliefs and perceptions of the problem, and the making plans to effectively cope. Clients should be encouraged to commit to follow through on plans to avert a recurrence or deepening of the crisis. Simple, specific action-plan goals should be mutually set that can achieve and maintain the client's sense of balance and equilibrium. For example, daily routines and habits that the client suspended during the onset of the crisis may be re-established. Daily walks, meditations, journaling, relaxation exercises, support group meetings, work-related activities, hobbies and other interests should be specifically discussed and a commitment made to re-engage in them. Several sessions may be required to explore the issues in this stage and to establish balance and equilibrium.

Stage 4 may occur over several sessions with exploration of the precipitating event, the series of "hazardous" events that led to the client's vulnerability, and the client's response.

Stage 5 — Focused Problem Solving

Stage 5 is entered as the crisis itself appears to have subsided to the point that the client has brought some sense of normalcy and relief into his or her life. The goal of stage 5 is to explore the main problem that led to the crisis by looking at the cumulation of behavioral responses the individual made that contributed to the crisis itself. The way to visualize this is as follows. The beginning of a crisis intervention can be viewed as overcoming a major obstacle or barrier that can lead to more severe problems. *The major obstacle that is encountered is the client's deep feelings about the crisis* (or the precipitating event). Once the obstacle has been overcome and the serious, disruptive feelings have subsided, *more relevant problem solving strategies can be employed that build resilience* to future problems and lead to better decision-making.

In stage 5, there is *exploration of similar crisis events* in the client's life. The precipitating events themselves, how and why the client was vulnerable to them, and their behavioral responses are explored. *Patterns* will emerge showing why hazardous conditions and vulnerable states occur with particular clients. Next, a *brainstorming of options* — behavioral possibilities in response to precipitating events — is conducted. The counselor may be forced to provide the client with some options, but, in general, the client should be encouraged to think of possibilities. *Each option is thought through to "see where it could*

The goal of stage 5 is to explore the main problem that led to the crisis by looking at the cumulation of behavioral responses the individual made that contributed to the crisis itself.

---

lead." As this is done, the client will come to understand how he or she can be less vulnerable, employ preventative measures, and more appropriately respond to problems when they do occur. Making plans for beneficial change and restoring the client's sense of control are primary concerns. *The client should be encouraged to develop and follow through with plans to correct and modify particular behaviors and habits that lead to vulnerability and hazardous conditions.* Remaining sober, developing support systems, rectifying problem relationships, establishing appropriate work/school habits, maintaining physical and emotional balance, and other related areas are focused upon.

One consistent finding in crisis intervention research has been that many clients appear more amenable to other treatment interventions when a crisis has been successfully mastered. Thus, crises can be an opportunity to stimulate and encourage needed major changes in the client's life. However, during the crisis, the focus of crisis intervention is on the factors involved with the crisis itself. As the crisis subsides, other relevant issues can be probed.

The client should be encouraged to develop and follow through with plans to correct and modify particular behaviors and habits that lead to vulnerability and hazardous conditions. Remaining sober, developing support systems, rectifying problem relationships, establishing appropriate work/school habits, maintaining physical and emotional balance, and other related areas are focused upon.

Specific Crisis Issues
Frequently Encountered

A core of specific crises will tend to occur with clients in treatment. All of the events on the life stressor list presented in an earlier section can precipitate crises. The following is a list of some crises frequently encountered along with specific crisis intervention hints.

Medical Emergencies (Including Possible Overdose)

Unless the individual faces danger from their location, don't move them until the extent of the emergency and their condition is known. Send for medical help, but don't leave the client alone. Try to find out what the person has taken if an overdose is possible — look around the person for clues for what drug might have been taken. Remain calm and provide assurance to the person that help is on the way. Provide appropriate support through calm discussion, ask specific yes/no questions, address the client by his or her name, and touch him/her if appropriate or necessary. If the person goes to the hospital, have someone the client trusts (including yourself if possible) go along.

Violent Clients

In situations where a client is obviously violent or dangerous, do not try to overpower him or her without sufficient help. Institutions should contain violent persons only with sufficient personnel to easily manage the situation. When faced with overwhelming odds, most violence-threatening clients will back down. If force is used, only use the force

---

If force is used, only use the force necessary to restrain.

---

necessary to restrain. Armed clients should be avoided and the police called. If you are directly faced by an armed client, remain calm and follow the client's instructions (to save your life as well as other's lives). Many police departments have a mental health response team designed for this purpose.

As clients become increasingly agitated, many will talk rapidly and make violent gestures. Counselors should calmly assure the client that things will be all right and to calm down. Keep a calm, relaxed voice tone. Remember the primary goals of crisis intervention's initial stages when faced with angry clients. You are seeking to relieve pressure and reduce anxiety and pressure. So remain calm, don't feel intimidated, don't make threats, and control the situation so that others don't escalate the problem.

Predictors of Violence

The best predictor of future behavior is past behavior. Therefore, it is known that perpetrators of past violence are likely candidates to perform future violent acts. In addition,

The best predictor of future behavior is past behavior. Therefore, it is known that perpetrators of past violence are likely candidates to perform future violent acts. In addition, clients who have been recently violent show elevated risks for current violence. Clients with the diagnosis of Antisocial Personality Disorder are the most prone to violence.

clients who have been recently violent show elevated risks for current violence. Clients with the diagnosis of Antisocial Personality Disorder are the most prone to violence. Many batterers, bullies, frequently angry and loudly intimidating clients will show this diagnosis. In addition, some mental health patients show sudden, irrational violence with little provocation. Programs should have firm policies and procedures regarding violence and the consequences of it. These policies and procedures should be completely explained to clients at program entry and at other routine times.

It is important to remember that treatment programs can have an underlying level of tension due to various factors — including tension between clients. Use good sense and judgement in making room and roommate assignments.

Depression/Suicidal Clients

Since suicidal clients are an extremely important issue, prior sections have addressed this issue. Always assess the risks of potential suicide. Asking the three assessment questions presented earlier can help with this. Using another assessment

---

Always assess the risks of potential suicide. ... Using another assessment inventory like the Beck Depression Inventory can also be useful. Contrary to popular belief, some people who threaten suicide repeatedly actually do carry it out. Suicide can sometimes be seen by clients as a way out of an intolerable, unmanageable situation.

---

inventory like the Beck Depression Inventory can also be useful. Contrary to popular belief, some people who threaten suicide repeatedly actually do carry it out. Suicide can sometimes be seen by clients as a way out of an intolerable, unmanageable situation. Thus, when faced with such clients, counselors should immediately employ crisis intervention. If there is a a genuine, high risk of suicide despite the initial crisis intervention, counselors should notify appropriate authorities. If possible, seek advice from a supervisor or senior staff members.

Relapse

Relapse can present a crisis for many clients. Some clients will come to believe that "all is lost" after a relapse and develop deep guilt and failure feelings. Some will think, "I might as well go all the way."

Hopefully your program will employ relapse prevention programming that can allow clients to see relapse as a learning experience — an opportunity to learn more about their addiction and themselves. If relapse is treated as a crisis, the initial stage is to help the client's deep feelings of anxiety and tension subside. Thus, assuring the client that "all is not lost" is important. For example, some clients will see their sobriety date as an all or nothing date. They may say, "I've been clean and sober for 5 years and now it's gone because I drank last night." A counselor can reply, "if you remain clean and

---

If relapse is treated as a crisis, the initial stage is to help the client's deep feelings of anxiety and tension subside. Thus, assuring the client that "all is not lost" is important.

---

sober today, tomorrow you can say you've been clean and sober for five years and a day out of the last five years and two days." Remember that relapse has upset the equilibrium of the client and that restoration of sobriety and sober behavior can help restore the balance. As to the specific goal that can be set, going to support group meetings and making it through the day clean and sober are appropriate.

Job Loss - Financial Problems

Substance abusers frequently "lose" jobs. Helping them get over their initial anxieties and tensions about the loss can prepare them to take appropriate action steps to gain control over this important life area. As with relapse prevention, the loss of a job can be viewed as an opportunity. Many substance abusers lack the education and experience to even get a job that meets their level of ability and interest. After the crisis intervention counselor helps the client manage and control their anger, frustration, and initial anxiety, the next step can be mobilizing various resources to assist in basic life skills management. For example, almost all communities have agencies that assist families with housing, utilities, basic necessities, medical care,

---

Many substance abusers lack the education and experience to even get a job that meets their level of ability and interest. After the crisis intervention counselor helps the client manage and control their anger, frustration, and initial anxiety, the next step can be mobilizing various resources to assist in basic life skills management.

---

and financial aid/management. After some limited plans are made to control the current financial crisis, problem solving efforts can take place that address the underlying problem. Ask the client how they can avert this problem in the future? Ask them what kind of job will give them what they want and will be most satisfying? How can they get the education and experience required for this job? What resources are available that can assist them in this process? What are the action steps needed to achieve it?

Death of a Loved One — Serious Illness

Grief is a normal human reaction that everyone faces. Most clients go through a series of predictable stages in grief or when a serious illness has been diagnosed. These are denial, anger, bargaining, depression, and acceptance. In **denial**, the person simply refuses to see reality. **Anger** follows the breakdown of denial and the individual poses the question, "why me?" Some clients in crisis enter crisis counseling with anger and resentment. At this stage, listening and understanding the client's statements are important. In the **bargaining** stage clients may pose hypothetical situations to try to gain time. They may state that if they straighten up maybe the person will get better. Guilt is often an underlying emotion. **Depression** typically follows when bargaining doesn't work or when it is apparent that the individual has little or no control over the situation. Simply allowing the client to express their feelings to

---

Most clients go through a series of predictable stages in grief or when a serious illness has been diagnosed. These are denial, anger, bargaining, depression, and acceptance.

---

an accepting, comforting counselor is appropriate. **Acceptance** occurs when the individual is resigned to the loss and is typified by some withdrawal. Support, understanding, and empathy are appropriate at this stage.

Loss of an Important Relationship

Many abusers in treatment undergo the loss of important relationships during the treatment process. In general, the same stages occur here as occur in grief. Denial may occur first followed by anger. Some clients who are angry may express the wish to retaliate and strike back. Processing these feelings by listening and reflecting them can assist the client in moving through the stages. The bargaining stage may be apparent when the individual makes desperate attempts to hold on to their relationship by trying to make deals, promising to straighten up, or just trying to buy more time. Counselors should note that many batterers can be very effective at bargaining with their victims to give them "one more chance." They effectively employ guilt, threats, and other power and control strategies to keep their victim under their control.

Many abusers in treatment undergo the loss of important relationships during the treatment process... Counselors should note that many batterers can be very effective at bargaining with their victims to give them "one more chance." They effectively employ guilt, threats, and other power and control strategies to keep their victim under their control.

Offender Crises

Offenders have many of the same crises as discussed with substance abusers. In addition, there are a few other situations that merit discussion.

Adjustment to Incarceration

As discussed in prior sections, many offenders will go through a time-limited adjustment period immediately after incarceration. Note that this adjustment reaction will often occur when housing assignments are changed and when their place of confinement changes. Programs and correctional counseling staff should endeavor to provide screenings, adequate orientations where all questions and concerns are at least heard by staff, and the provision of some support is made to those who show obvious needs. Providing offenders with rules, procedures, schedules of activities, and possible options during their incarceration can increase their sense of control.

Fear/Threats

Crises in institutions can occur when offenders are threatened by others or simply fearful. One reason that prison gangs have proliferated is the perceived lack of social support systems in the facility. Gangs can provide a sense of security

Providing offenders with rules, procedures, schedules of activities, and possible options during their incarceration can increase their sense of control.

and support. Thus, developing alternative, appropriate institutional support systems is important. Regular support groups
like AA, NA, religious groups, educational groups, and discussion clubs can provide support. Offenders who are or feel
threatened should be assessed for possible housing assignment
changes to alleviate possible problems.

Problems With Staff

While it is not appropriate, it is true that some staff
members in institutions can "pick on" specific offenders causing
crises. Offenders must realize that there is an appropriate
process to make complaints about such situations, but in reality, their complains may not be acted on. Regular staff meetings
involving all staff can assist in gaining the cooperation of key
staff, but ultimately the offender must realize that they can only
control their own actions. After listening to the offender and

> *...developing alternative, appropriate institutional support systems is important. Regular support groups like AA, NA, religious groups, educational groups, and discussion clubs can provide support. Offenders who are or feel threatened should be assessed for possible housing assignment changes to alleviate possible problems.*

understanding their feelings, allowing them to ventilate, follow the basic crisis intervention stages. Have the offender make small, appropriate goals and gradually build to real problem-solving. The focus of this must be on their behavior — not the behavior of the staff member.

...it is true that some staff members in institutions can "pick on" specific offenders causing crises. Offenders must realize that there is an appropriate process to make complaints about such situations... ultimately the offender must realize that they can only control their own actions. After listening to the offender and understanding their feelings, allowing them to ventilate, follow the basic crisis intervention stages.

Have the offender make small, appropriate goals and gradually build to real problem-solving. The focus of this must be on their behavior — not the behavior of the staff member.

Parole/Probation Loss

Not being granted parole or probation can cause crises in offenders. Many offenders teach others the philosophy, "hope for the best but plan for the worst" when meeting parole boards. It is important that staff not give false hopes to clients — especially when the client perceives so much "riding" on a particular hearing. Offenders should approach such hearings prepared to give it their best shot, but also understand that many factors influence release decisions — including inmate populations, public perceptions, victim's statements, and even the mood of hearing officers. The offender must realize that the only thing they control is their behavior. So they should do their best but also accept that some things are out of their control.

> **The offender must realize that the only thing they control is their behavior. So they should do their best but also accept that some things are out of their control.**

REFERENCES

Bartolucci, G., & Drayer, C. S. (1973) An overview of crisis intervention in the emergency rooms of general hospitals. *American Journal of Psychiatry*, 130, 953-960.

Berlin, I. (1970) Crisis intervention and short-term therapy: an approach in a child psychiatric clinic. *Journal of Child Psychiatry*, 9, 595-606.

Butcher, J., N., & Maudal, G. R. (1976) Crisis intervention. In: I. B. Weiner (Ed.) *Clinical Methods in Psychology*. New York: Wiley.

Caplan, G. (1960) Patterns of parent response to the crisis of premature birth. *Psychiatry*, 23, 365-374.

Caplan, G. (1964) *Principles of Preventative Psychiatry*. New York: Basic Books.

Ewalt, P. L. (1973) The crisis-treatment approach in a child guidance clinic. *Social Casework*, 54, 406-411.

Gilliland, B. E., & James, R. K. (1988) *Crisis Intervention Strategies*. Pacific Grove, CA: Brooks/Cole.

Hoffman, D. L., & Remmel, M. L. (1975) Uncovering the precipitant in crisis intervention. *Social Casework*, 56, 259-267.

Kaffman, M. (1963) Short-term family therapy. *Family Process*, 2.

Kardener, S. H. (1975) A methodologic approach to crisis therapy. *American Journal of Psychotherapy*, 29, 4-13.

Lang, J. 1974) Planned short-term treatment in a family agency. *Social Casework*, 55, 369-374.

Lindemann, E. (1944) Symptomatology and management of acute grief. *American Journal of Psychiatry*, 101, 141-148.

Parad, H. J., & Caplan, G. (1960) A framework for studying families in crisis. *Journal of Social Work*, 5, 3-15.

Patterson, V., & O'Sullivan, M. (1974) Three perspectives on brief psychotherapy. *American Journal of Psychotherapy*, 28, 265-277.

Rapoport, L. (1962) The state of crisis: some theoretical considerations. *Social Service Review*, 36.

Schwartz, S. L. (1971) A review of crisis intervention programs. *Psychiatric Quarterly*, 45, 498-508.

Shaw, R., Blumenfeld, H., & Snef, R. (1968) A short-term treatment program in a child guidance clinic. *Social Work*, 13, 81-90.

Taplin, J. R. (1971) Crisis theory: critique and reformulation. *Community Mental Health Journal*, 7, 13-24.

Waldfogel, S., & Gardner, G. E. (1961) Intervention in crises as a method of primary prevention. In: G. Caplan (Ed.) *The Prevention of Mental Disorders in Children*, New York: Basic Books.

Wolkon, G. H. (1972) Crisis theory, the application for treatment, and dependency. *Comprehensive Psychiatry*, 13, 459-464.

APPENDIX A

Crisis Intervention Guide Forms

The following guide may be copied by purchasers of this book and utilized as client forms or as a simple reference to crisis intervention.

CRISIS INTERVENTION GUIDE
Adapted from Little, Robinson, & Burnette (1998)

This form may be used to structure crisis intervention sessions and as a guide or primer for use with clients.

Client Name: _____ Age:_____ Sex: _____

Marital Status: _____

Program Status:_____

Counselor:_____Date of session: ____Time of session:_____

Stage 1 — Crisis Recognition

a) How did the crisis come to the counselor's attention?

b) Does the crisis appear to be life threatening?

c) Was medical care necessary?

d) Briefly describe the client's affect at the beginning of the session (feelings & emotions):

e) Briefly describe the client's behavior at the beginning of the session:

f) What was the client's response to the counselor's initial questions? (*What is going on?," "is there something I can do?,"* or *"would you like to talk about this?"*)

1

Hint: The goal of this initial intervention is to assist the client to make positive behavioral actions to resolve the crisis and *prevent relapse, injury, or further harm.* Keep the client feeling safe. Simply engaging the client in a discussion and attending to their problem can provide some immediate relief. In addition, talking to the counselor about the problem represents a positive behavioral action by the client. After this has been accomplished, move to the next stage.

Stage 2 — Define The Problem

Hint: *Listening* to the client's story, truly *understanding* what they say both *verbally* and through *nonverbal* behavior, and to letting the client know that the counselor hears and understands are important. This may take some time and requires giving the client *feedback*, occasionally seeking *clarification*, and *restating* what the client says to validate that the counselor hears and understands what is being said. The goal here is to understand *what has caused the crisis, why the client feels vulnerable and unable to cope with it, and possible ramifications of the crisis.* Counselors facilitate this by *asking simple, direct questions.*

a) Define the precipitating event by asking: what *brought on this crisis?*

b) Ask: *how and when did this event occur?*

c) Ask: *who else is involved?*

d) Ask: *what have you done about this as of now?*

e) What important responses were made to these questions (both verbal and nonverbal reactions)?

f) If the client is depressed* ask: *How depressed are you?*

g) If the client answers that they are fairly depressed or appear to be depressed ask, *do you have a plan?* (If the client doesn't understand, ask "do you know how you would kill yourself if you did it?")

h) If the client has a plan, ask a specific question based on their plan to assess if they have access to the means they would employ. For example, ask, *do you have access to a gun?*

*Hint: If there is a significant risk of suicide, you must make a decision on whether to notify others or make an agreement with the client. Within programs, you should let other staff know about it. In using the agreement, the client agrees to not do anything until they have talked to you first. With suicidal and severely depressed clients, give them a telephone number where you can be reached and the number of a crisis center.

i) When you have a real understanding of the problem situation, begin formulating a simple plan of action by moving to state 3.

Stage 3 — Assist In The Setting of a Limited Goal

Hint: After the client's precipitating event is understood and the counselor understands how this has affected the client, *a limited goal that is related to the problem and is easily attainable should be mutually set.* *Averting a deeper crisis* and bringing a sense of *balance* back into the client's life are goals here. Clients need *respect* and *concern* rather than blame or guilt, but the counselor should be directive in the setting of the goal.

a) What goal can be agreed to that can be easily accomplished and relates to the client's problem:

b) Will the client agree to fulfill the goal?

c) When and how will the goal be accomplished?

d) Have you "pinned down" all aspects of the goal so that there will be no misunderstandings?

e) When will the client meet with you again?

Hint: *Remember that an overriding goal of the initial session is to protect the client, protect others, prevent relapse, and alleviate unbearable pressures.* If this goal has been achieved, set another appointment time immediately after the goal is scheduled to be accomplished. While there is some flexibility with the next meeting, it should be *as soon as is possible* keeping in mind that some crises can be life-threatening and/or relapse producing. Counselors who are skilled in relaxation exercises and anxiety reducing methods may find these useful to employ at this time.

f) Are there any other strategies (relaxation techniques) that you can or should employ before ending the initial session?

g) Does the client know how to reach you if the crisis worsens?

h) If there are outside support systems available to the client, have they been discussed? (What are they?)

i) Has the client agreed to employ their outside support systems?

j) Has the client's anxiety and tension levels decreased to the point where they can be responsibly released from the session?

Stage 4 — Beginning Problem Solving Efforts & Support

Hint: With completion of the limited goal from the prior stage, many clients will experience a lessening of anxiety and tension. At the same time, *clients need ongoing encouragement and need to see that they have the ability to resolve and make it through the crisis. How the crisis involves other people, how much it impacts the client's significant others, and the effects of the crisis on the client can be explored.* Maintain the basic counseling approach of *listening and attending, restating and paraphrasing to validate the counselor's understanding of the problem, and allowing the client to express emotions and feelings.*

a) Did the client do the goal from last session?

b) What is the status of the crisis now?

c) Have you discussed how some reactions to crises are normal?

d) Did the client utilize any of their outside support systems?

e) How does the client view their problem?

f) Why does the client feel vulnerable?

g) How do significant others view their problem?

h) What options are available to them?

i) Will the client agree to re-establish daily routines and habits (e.g., walking, journaling, meetings, etc.) that gave them a sense of balance prior to the crisis?

j) Ask: **What we can do about this problem?**

k) Begin to form an action plan by setting a few more easily attainable goals and have the client agree to them.

l) Does the client know when their next session is and what is expected of them prior to the next session?

Hint: In this stage of crisis counseling, the major focus of sessions will be on exploration of the current crisis, current support systems, client beliefs and perceptions of the problem, and the making plans to effectively cope. Several sessions may be devoted to the stage 4 formula.

Stage 5 — Focused Problem Solving

Hint: The goal of stage 5 is to explore the main problem that led to the crisis by looking at the cumulation of behavioral responses the individual made that contributed to the crisis itself. The beginning of crisis intervention can be viewed as overcoming a major obstacle or barrier that can lead to more severe problems. *The major obstacle that is encountered is the client's deep feelings about the crisis* (or the precipitating event). Once the obstacle has been overcome and the serious, disruptive feelings have subsided, *more relevant problem solving strategies can be employed that build resilience* to future problems and lead to better decision-making.

a) What similar crises have occurred in the client's life?

b) How were these handled by the client?

c) Why was the client either vulnerable or not vulnerable to these crises?

d) Is there a pattern or consistency in these events and their response?

e) What are all of the possible options available to the client if future crises occur that are similar to this one?

f) What are the consequences of these options?

g) What are the best options open to the client?

h) What plans can be made with the client to reduce their vulnerability?

i) Does the crisis appear to have subsided?

j) Is the client more resilient to future crises?

APPENDIX B

Anxiety & Depression Scales

The following noncopyrighted tests may be used to assess anxiety and depression in clients. The forms may be reproduced. Answers and scoring on each question are based on an interview with the client. Clients should not self administer the tests, but rather, the questions should be asked during the interview.

The Anxiety Status Inventory

The **Anxiety Status Inventory** reference is: Zung, Wm. W. K., A rating instrument for anxiety disorders, *Psychosomatics* (1971), 12, 371-379. It is used to assess anxiety neurosis. It is a 20-item test that rates from 1 (none) to 4 (severe). Scores range from 20 to 80. Research indicates that the **mean raw score** for anxiety disorder is 49.5; personality disorders average 41.6; depressive disorders average 39.9; transient situational disorders average 33.5. *The test is not used to diagnose* but should be used as part of an overall clinical interview to assess severity of anxiety. The intensity and duration of the symptom addressed in each item should be evaluated. When the symptom is not present or is insignificant in duration or intensity, rate it **None** (score = 1). If it is present occasionally, rate it **Mild** (score = 2). If it is present a "good part of the time," rate it **Moderate** (score = 3). If it is "present most or all of the time, rate it **Severe** (score = 4). You should ask questions like, "How bad was it?; How long did it last?; How much of the time did it occur?"

The Anxiety Status Inventory

Client Name:_____ Date:_____

Anxiety Symptom	Interview Questions	Score ↓
1. Anxiousness	Do you ever feel nervous and anxious?	
2. Fear	Have you ever felt afraid?	
3. Panic	How easily do you get upset? Have you ever had panic spells?	
4. Mental disintegration	Do you ever feel like you are going to pieces or falling apart?	
5. Apprehension	Have you ever felt uneasy or that something terrible was going to happen?	
6. Tremors	Have you found yourself trembling or shaking?	
7. Somatic problems	Do you have headaches, neck or back pains?	
8. Weakness	How easily do you get tired or weak?	
9. Restlessness	Do you get restless and can't sit still?	
10. Palpitation	Have you ever felt your heart was running away?	
11. Dizziness	Do you ever have dizzy spells?	
12. Faintness	Do you have fainting spells or feel like it?	
13. Breathing	Do you ever have trouble with your breathing?	
14. Paresthesias	Do you have numbness or tingling in your fingers or mouth?	
15. Nausea	Do you ever feel sick to your stomach or feel like vomiting?	
16. Urinary	How often do you need to empty your bladder?	
17. Sweating	Do you ever get wet, clammy hands?	
18. Flushing	Do you ever feel your face get hot or blush?	
19. Insomnia	How have you been sleeping?	
20. Nightmares	Do you have dreams that scare you?	
	TOTAL SCORE =	

The Depression Status Inventory

The **Depression Status Inventory** reference is: Zung, Wm. W. K., The Depression Status Inventory: An adjunct to the self-rating depression scale, *Journal of Clinical Psychology* (1972), 28, 539-543. It is used to assess depression and anxiety neurosis. It is a 20-item test that rates from 1 (none) to 4 (severe). Scores range from 20 to 80. Research indicates that the **mean raw score** for depression disorder is 49; personality disorders average 41.5; anxiety disorders average 41; transient situational disorders average 35. *The test is not used to diagnose* but should be used as part of an overall clinical interview to assess severity of depression. The intensity and duration of the symptom addressed in each item should be evaluated. When the symptom is not present or is insignificant in duration or intensity, rate it **None** (score = 1). If it is present occasionally, rate it **Mild** (score = 2). If it is present a "good part of the time," rate it **Moderate** (score = 3). If it is "present most or all of the time, rate it **Severe** (score = 4). You should ask questions like, "How bad was it?; How long did it last?; How much of the time did it occur?"

The Depression Status Inventory

Client Name:_____ Date:_____

Depression Symptom	Interview Questions	Score▼
1. Depressed mood	Do you ever feel sad or depressed?	
2. Crying spells	Do you ever have crying spells or feel like it?	
3. Daily variation	Is there any part of the day you feel worse or best?	
4. Sleep disturbance	Do you have frequent and early morning awakenings?	
5. Decreased appetite	How is your appetite?	
6. Weight loss	Have you lost any weight?	
7. Decreased libido	Do you enjoy looking, talking or being with attractive men/women?	
8. Constipation	Do you have trouble with constipation?	
9. Tachycardia	Have you had times when your heart was beating faster than usual?	
10. Fatigue	How easily do you get tired?	
11. Movement agitation	Do you find yourself restless and can't sit still?	
12. Movement retardation	Do you feel slowed down in doing the things you usually do?	
13. Confusion	Do you ever feel confused and have trouble thinking?	
14. Emptiness	Do you feel life is empty for you?	
15. Hopelessness	How hopeful do you feel about the future?	
16. Indecisiveness	How are you at making decisions?	
17. Irritability	Do easily do you get irritated?	
18. Dissatisfaction	Do you still enjoy the things you used to?	
19. Personal devaluation	Do you ever feel useless and not wanted?	
20. Suicidal rumination	Have you had thoughts about doing away with yourself?	
	TOTAL SCORE =	

INDEX

Active crisis ...12
Antisocial personality disorder ...33-34
Anxiety ...3, 13, 17, 29, 35, 36
Bartolucci, G. ...6
Batterers ...34
Berlin, I. ...5
Blumenfeld, H. ...5
Butcher, J. ...4, 5
Caplan, Gerald ...1-7
Chemical abusers and crisis intervention ...8
Coconut Grove fire ...1
Cognitive model ...6
Crises (types — developmental/accidental) ...2, 7
Crisis as brief psychotherapy ...4-5
Crisis counseling ...20-31
Crisis intervention definition ...7, 9
Denial ...37
Depression ...22, 34-35
Drayer, C. ...6
Duration of crises ... 2
DWI ...8, 17
Eclectic model ...7
Equilibrium model ...6
Emotional reactions to crises ...2
Erikson, Erik ... 1, 7
Ewalt, P. ...5
Factors in crises ...10
Family involvement in crises ...5
Fear/threats ...39-40
Financial problems ...36-37
Gardner G. ...4, 5
Gilliland, B. ...6, 7
Goals ...18, 22, 23-27, 28

Grief reactions/stages ...1, 28, 37-38
Hazardous event ...10, 29, 31
Helplessness ...11
History 1-3
Hoffman, D. ...5, 6
Homeostasis ... 2
Interpretation of crisis ...2
Irrational beliefs and crisis ...6
James, R. ...6, 7
Job loss ...36-37
Kaffman, M. ...5
Kardener, S....5
Lang, J. ...5
Lindemann, Erich ...1
Maudal, G. ...4, 5
Medical emergencies ...32
Mental disorders and crisis ...3
Offenders and crisis intervention ...8, 9, 12-13, 39-42
O'Sullivan M. ...4, 5
Overdose ...32
Parad, H. ...4
Past experience and crises ...4
Patterson, V. ...4, 5
Precipitating event ...5, 11, 12, 22, 29, 30
Preventive crisis intervention ...1
Psychosocial transition model ...7
Rahe, Richard ...14
Rapoport, L. ...4
Relapse ...9, 13, 21, 25, 35-36
Relationship loss ...38
Remmel, M. ...5, 6
Schwartz, S. ...5
Senf, R. ...5
Shaw, R. ...5
Social group (as factor in crisis) ...3
Stages of crisis ...1, 2-3, 12-13

Stressors (in life) ...14-15, (offenders; 16-19)
Suicide ...17, 22-23, 25-26, 34-35
Taplin, J. ...6
Threats ...2
Tension (see anxiety)
Trial and error (efforts to solve crises) ...3, 13
Violence ...32-34
Vulnerability ...11, 29, 31
Waldfogel, S. ...4, 5
Wellesley Human Relations Service ...1
Wolkon, G. ...5

ABOUT THE AUTHORS

Dr. Gregory L. Little received his Doctor of Education Degree in Counseling and a Master of Science Degree in Psychology from the University of Memphis and is a Licensed Professional Counselor. He is a trainer for Advanced Training Associates and Correctional Counseling, Inc. and is Editor of *Cognitive Behavioral Treatment Review*. He also teaches in Louisiana State University at Shreveport's substance abuse certification program. Dr. Little is author of the books *The Archetype Experience* (1984), *People of the Web* (1990), *Grand Illusions* (1994), *Staying Quit: A Cognitive-Behavioral Relapse Prevention Guide* (1997), and *Psychopharmacology* (1997). He is also co-author of all of the MRT® treatment materials and other books including *Effective Counseling Approaches for Chemical Abusers and Offenders, How To Escape Your Prison, Your Inner Enemy, Filling The Inner Void, Character Development, Family Support, Job Readiness, Parenting and Family Values, Understanding & Treating The Antisocial Substance Abuser, Discovering Life & Liberty in the Pursuit of Happiness, Coping With Anger,* and *Bringing Peace To Relationships*.

Dr. Kenneth D. Robinson received his Doctor of Education Degree in Educational Psychology and Counseling and a Master of Science Degree in Psychology from the University of Memphis. He is the President of Correctional Counseling, Inc. and is the co-developer of Moral Reconation Therapy (MRT®). He is Executive Editor of *Cognitive Behavioral Treatment Review*. He was Director of Clinical Services and Director of the Crisis Stabilization Unit for Midtown Mental Health Center in Memphis, Tennessee and also worked in Mental Health Services for the Shelby County Correction Center from 1975-1987. Dr. Robinson conducts frequent training and workshops in MRT® throughout the United States. He has published and presented numerous professional articles in the areas of mental health and treatment issues. He is co-author of all of the MRT® treatment materials and other books including *Effective Counseling Approaches, How To Escape Your Prison, Your Inner Enemy, Filling The Inner Void, Character Development, Family Support, Job Readiness, Understanding & Treating The Antisocial Substance Abuser, Parenting and Family Values, Discovering Life & Liberty in the Pursuit of Happiness, Coping With Anger,* and *Bringing Peace To Relationships*.

Katherine D. Burnette holds a Master of Science Degree in Psychology from the University of Memphis and is a licensed substance abuse counselor. She is Vice President of Clinical Services for Correctional Counseling, Inc. and conducts a variety of MRT® and other trainings in the United States. She served as a supervising counselor and interim Director of the Drug Offender Rehabilitation Program at the Shelby County Correction Center for over 7 years. Ms. Burnette has numerous research publications and is the coauthor of *Effective Counseling Approaches for Chemical Abusers and Offenders*.